# *MooDooM*

## *The 24 Streets of MooDooM*

| | | | |
|---|---|---|---|
| Street A: | Alcohol | Street N: | Neuroses |
| Street B: | Benzedrine | Street O: | Overdose |
| Street C: | Cocaine | Street P: | Peyote |
| Street D: | Dependency | Street Q: | Quitters |
| Street E: | Ecstasy | Street R: | Rehabilitation |
| Street F: | Fentanyl | Street S: | Sex |
| Street G: | Greed | Street T: | Tolerance |
| Street H: | Heroin | Street U: | User |
| Street I: | Illness | Street V: | Valium |
| Street J: | Jealousy | Street W: | Withdrawal |
| Street K: | Killing | Street XYZ: | (Exit Bridge) |
| Street L: | L.S.D. | | |
| Street M: | Marijuana | | |

The first sign of MooDooM is the smell. It clings to the air like flies cling to shit. MooDooM has the rancid smell of decay. A putrid waste that defiles all that it touches. The source of this smell is a smoldering lake that sits in a valley, below the peak of a towering mountain.

Contraré descended that mountain. Entry to MooDooM begins with crossing the River of Addiction. An estuary of pain that encircles the city. A rank repository of waste that flows through the streets of a vast city that stretches beyond any sight. With such an enormous area Contraré would need luck to find his Mary Shelley. But trusting the luck of a hunch and hoping for some grace, he entered one of MooDooM's 24 Streets.

Contraré crossed the River of Addiction onto Alcohol Street. It was an uneventful crossing for all are welcome on Alcohol Street. It is when one tries to leave, that the trouble begins. Quickly assimilating with a crowd of moving faces, he tried to get an intuitive feel for which way to turn. Going both right and then left he walked about as if in a daze until he gradually honed in on something that felt familiar. A place that held his Mary Shelley.

It was the type of bar you find with only a number for its name. Passing through a darkened doorway, he stopped to let his eyes adjust to the darkness. Eyes that viewed a smoke coated room, dimly lit by a smoldering fireplace in the corner. Contraré instinctively knew from the smell that caution was a prudent path. Dank smells of spilt beer and foul piss indiscriminately choked the air.

He sensed that Mary Shelley was here. Moving cautiously to an empty corner of the room, Contraré

# *MooDooM*

*By*

*Contraré DGaul*

*2020 Edition MeoPian
Publishing 138 Elkin Ave*

*Indiana, PA 15701*

MooDooM

Copyright © 2021 By Contraré DGaul

adjusted his posture to mimic the look of everyone else. Dropping his chin and hunching his shoulders, be found the bar to be moderately occupied with more than ten, but less than twenty customers. Crusty looking people that were barely alive, as they nursed their drinks for companionship.

It was a pathetic place of extreme disparities that breed contempt and jealousy between the have and the have nots. Feelings that change a place as they creep from the gutters and fester in the minds of men. Tormented people that shuffled across the room with a labored intensity, resembling the submissive resignation of a forced death march.

And then she appeared. A Magical Princess working as a petite young waitress. A Maiden of Softness somehow changed for she was different. Her demeanor now exaggerated and strained. She moved with the burden of excessive exposure to Addiction. Spotting Contraré from across the room, Mary Shelley graciously approached.

"What can I get you?" She asked.

"I have to get you out of here Mary Shelley!"

"I am not going anywhere."

"Please Mary Shelley, do not be difficult. I have to get you back."

"But I am not ready to go. I will be off of work soon. Relax and have a drink. Then we can talk."

"Okay, whiskey and a beer." He spoke with a rehearsed flair.

An order she accepted with a slight smile and

staggering turn that moved across the room. A troubled young maiden with light skin, long black hair, and large oval eyes. Eyes that were sadly changed from the Mary Shelley of before. Struggling to assuredly carry her small build, she cautiously ushered the drinks along.

"That will be five dollars. Anything else?"

Slowly reaching into his shirt, Contraré pulled a wrinkled bill from his breast pocket. One of many bills, for he never went anywhere without money and never carried it in less than three places.

"No that will be quite enough, until I decide how to get us out of here Mary Shelley."

"My name is not Mary Shelley. My name is Gabriela!"

"When did that happen?"

"When I came here. Everything changes in this place. I am not the person you once knew. That person is gone. She has changed. I am now Gabriela. Dancer of the streets!"

"Okay Gabriela. What do you want to do?"

"A lot of things, but not in public. Let me try something safe. Would you like me to read your Tarot?"

"This is not the time for a Tarot reading."

"I think it is the perfect time. Come on. It will be fun."

"Okay Gabriela, whatever you want."

"Thanks." She said with a smile while crossing to retrieve her Tarot.

It was during this period of musing over the circumstances, that two shadowy men slithered through the doorway. The one was tall and the other short, although both looked drawn. A hollowed thinness that comes from struggling with life.

Approaching them timidly, Gabriela avoided their stares and meekly took their order. Moving hastily to the bar, she prepared their drinks and grabbed her cards. Appearing uneasy in the presence of these men, she quietly served them before walking quickly to Contraré.

"Those guys are bad." She whispered.

"Do not worry. I will watch them for you."

"Thanks. So let us see what the cards have to predict."

Shuffling the cards end to end and then side to side, she repeated this pattern three times. Then she spoke a brief incantation; "Oh great power of the Tarot, share with us a glimpse of the future," and placed the deck before him.

"Tap the deck just one time." Gabriela instructed. Contraré complied and she spread the future before them.

## *Tarot Reading*

Position 1: The Tower

Position 2: Judgment

Position 3: The Fool

Position 4: The Empress

Position 5: Lovers

Position 6: The Hermit

Position 7: The Hanged Man

Position 8: The Devil

Position 9: The Moon

Position 10: The World

"What does it mean Mary Shelley? I mean Gabriela."

"Give me a minute, there is a lot here. We need to be very careful."

"You are making me uncomfortable Gabriela."

"Patience my love. For all that wait, good things shall pass."

"It means that greatness is near, but your judgment is still being watched. Reject foolish decisions. Your Empress loves you, but love may by-pass your solitary ways. The path that you choose will save or destroy you. Avoid temptation. Follow the Moon and you can find the world."

"Can you interpret that into something I can use?"

"It means that some negative energy has attached itself to your aura. We must act quickly before you are afflicted."

"So can we now leave?"

"Soon my love. The red bearded man with the black leather coat is my shift handler. I must clear it with him first."

Watching as the Tall and Short men became louder and more boisterous, Contraré sensed that there would be trouble. They had a look of recklessness that shrouded them in anger. Their overstated postures reflected an obvious disdain for reason, implying they were guilty of hate and condemned to spreading harm.

It began with a taunt as Gabriela walked toward the bar. Approaching her handler as he spoke to another patron, the Short man walked to the bar and put his arm around her. Shrieking with disbelief, she stepped aside and tried to minimize the situation.

"Pardon me, but I am not that kind of girl."

"Well, perhaps you can tell me exactly what type of girl you are?"

"The man at that table is my boyfriend." Gabriela explained.

"I am quite sure that he will not mind, you being the type of girl that you are. Now give me a little comfort before I grow troubled." He insisted while grabbing Gabriela by the ass.

Once more Gabriela broke his hold and moved away.

"Are you going to let that go on?" She earnestly asked her handler.

"What is the problem?" He asked.

"That jerk just grabbed me!"

"I thought you knew that was part of the job."

"Yes, but I always have the right to say no!"

"No, my little street dancer. You have the right to do whatever I say. Do you get it?"

"So, it seems that you are available after all." The Short Man said.

"You and me have just begun." He grunted while pulling her into his arms.

Trying to remain calm despite difficult circumstances, Gabriela casually redressed the matter in a soft-spoken manner. Words that served to fuel his intentions. Intentions made clear by a lustful set of hands that crept up her hemline. An animal roughness that laughed with carnal glee.

Valiantly resisting the affront, Gabriela slapped the man across his face. A desperate rebuttal to break loose or bear the consequences of a sickening alternative. Heroically fighting for liberty, she lost to a villainous person who was sanctified by hate. A person blessed in Hades as he returned laughter for the slap.

Contraré watched both men with extreme caution. The Shift Handler had disappeared and the Tall man began to clap. Contraré knew that it is always best to avoid confrontation while in MooDooM, but this time he would have to make it stop. His following actions were justified.

The clap became louder, more intense and malicious. Stirring the pot as the situation boiled, the Short man worked himself into a frenzy as Gabriela squirmed to get away. About to break loose, the Short man seized her by the waist and drew her close. Still wriggling for freedom, the man grabbed her hair, twisted back her chin and savagely slapped her. Then a short pause, followed by a sinister grin and a series of three more.

The assault drew blood from her lip and tears from her eyes. A shaken woman as Gabriela's posture bent and demeanor changed. She was beaten and in need of immediate help. Well fear not for chivalry lives.

"Let her go!" Contraré yelled.

Three simple words that came crashing in on the situation. A powerful assertion that was delivered with such conviction as to still the room. A room about to explode with tension as he delivered his qualifier;

"I mean now!"

Reacting to his interference, the two men slowly turned toward him. Men not accustomed to taking orders. More than words will be needed for this confrontation. The Tall man was the first to speak.

"Buddy, we are only trying to have some fun. Do you like to have fun?"

"No! I like nothing about this!"

"Come now Buddy, you look like a reasonable man."

"Well, you are very mistaken."

"Why be difficult? She is a whore. She may fight, but she likes it."

"Well let her go and see if she stays!"

"Why not mind your own business and leave us to ours?" The Short man yelled as Gabriela broke loose and ran behind the bar.

The situation had reached a dangerous standoff. The men were seated between Gabriela and the door. Contraré was in the corner, but blocked from Gabriela. No one could move. A stalemate held in check by Contraré's concealed right hand.

"Buddy."

"I am not your Buddy!" Contraré barked.

"Okay man." He spoke with a sneer.

"We have a bit of a dilemma here. My friend has been away for a very long time and he needs the comfort of a women. And of all the women in town, he wants that one, but you say he cannot have her."

"That's right. She belongs to me. We just want out. No trouble. No hard feelings. Just let us go." Contraré negotiated.

Words wasted on deaf ears, for there was no sway in the men before him. They were pillars of hate, permanently imprisoned in the lives they endured. A mounting impasse that was about to break.

It began with the Tall man cautiously rising from his chair. A movement so mechanical that it was far from natural and anything but innocent. A diversionary move that was designed to draw Contraré's attention, as the Short man dropped his right hand toward his boot. An aggressive action that precipitated a response.

Acting with justified calmness, Contraré crushed their hostile intentions with an expressionless face and a small revolver. Not bothering to remove the gun from his pocket, Contraré fired for center of mass. A tidy shot that sliced the air before lodging itself in the Short man's shoulder. Wincing with pain as he slumped to the floor, the Tall man broke for the bar.

He was a suspicious looking character that was

desperately tugging at his coat pocket. Contraré resolutely drew his gun, aimed from the hip at the moving shadow and fired with deliberate intent. A second shot as accurate as the first, exploding in the shadow's thigh, crippling him to the ground.

Cautiously watching for any sign of reprisal, Contraré and Gabriela saw their moment for escape. Mutual comprehension of the situation convinced them to depart quickly as the two men struggled to regain composure. They planned to put considerable distance between themselves as fast as possible. Backing out of the doorway before emerging onto the street, Contraré discovered that the streets were crowded and Gabriela had disappeared.

But where could she be? Gabriela exited the bar first and Contraré followed her a second later, but now she was gone. Contraré cringed with despair over her disappearance into this endless stream of tortured faces. And then a moment that seemed endless, was finally broken as her soft voice calmed the roar of that maddening crowd.

"I want to thank you." She insisted.

"Where did you go?" He answered.

"Do not question me about where I go!" Gabriela barked.

"Okay, calm down, but I was worried. We need to get out of here." He pressed.

"Yes I know, but first I have to get my stuff."

"Forget it Mary Shelley, I mean Gabriela! There is nothing here that you need. We must go now!" Contraré argued.

"I am not going anywhere without my stuff!" She stubbornly replied.

"Oh Gabriela, please don't be difficult."

"Not without my stuff."

"Well, where is it?" He dejectedly asked.

"Across town." She answered.

"Across town! Are you crazy? We are not walking across this town!" Contraré exploded.

"I want my stuff."

"Listen to me Honey, I have no Astral Power here. We have to climb up the mountain before my strength will return. It is not safe for us to be on these streets."

"Not without my stuff." She insisted.

"Fine. Fine! That is just fine!"

"Really?" She uttered in disbelief.

"No, it is not fine, but if we must go then let it be now."

"Oh Contraré I love you." An unforeseen set of events that charted a treacherous path. A solitary man with a girl on his arm, unable to predict the danger that lay ahead.

"So, what is your name?"

"You know my name Gabriela, or whoever you are."

"Yes, but I want to know your other name." She answered.

"Please Honey, no more games."

"Come on Contraré. I want to have some fun."

"There is no fun to be had on these streets."

"I promise to play fair."

"You never play fair Mary Shelley. You cheat as much as I let you get away with." Contraré argued.

"True, but you like the games sometimes.

"Yes, but not here and not now. Let me get you back and we will have plenty of time for games."

"Please. Pretty please. Pretty please with dancers on top!" She pleaded.

"You never quit. Always the focus, always the clown, always living in the moment. I love your quirkiness more than ever Gabriela."

"Is that a yes? Why I think it is. Contraré, I do believe you just said yes!"

"Okay, but please keep moving."

"So, what is your name Contraré?"

"Not this name thing again."

"Names are important. They tell a lot about people. They reflect where you are from, the type of family you have and your name is something you hear every day of your life." Gabriela explained.

"You are in rare form my dear Mary Shelley. I relinquish myself to your charm. My name is Juan."

"I like it! Juan what?" She probed.

"You certainly are inquisitive. My name is Juan Carlos... Never mind."

"Pleased to meet you, Juan Carlos. So where do you come from?"

"Where do any of us come from Mary Shelley?"

"Stop it Juan Carlos, you are not playing fair. I am Gabriela!"

"Whatever Gabriela, just keep moving." Contraré stressed while quickening the pace.

"So, what do you want out of life Juan Carlos?"

"To get across town, pick up your stuff, and get out of here without any more problems."

"Are you not going to ask me what I want Juan Carlos?"

"Okay, what do you want?" He tensely replied.

"I want a big house with pretty clothes and nice friends. I want a life of contentment, free to live and learn. And I want to love a man who gets what he wants and wants what he gets."

"You already have those things at home Mary Shelley. I mean Gabriela."

"Not anymore. That life is far away and I am troubled with the future."

"You will feel differently once I get you back home."

He insisted.

"Home. Such a funny word. It means a lot to those that have one, but only a word to those without." She lamented.

"Yes, Gabriela and we have a nice home that means a lot to you, so just hold onto that idea."

"You make it sound so simple. Just hold onto hope when all hope is gone. How do I do that? How do I hold onto a belief that I no longer believe?"

"Trust will and faith. Stay sober, trust me and try to believe."

"How long have I been here?" Gabriela inquired.

"A month. Part of you has been here since you fell out of the Zodiac Circle. It took seven days before you lost consciousness. That was three weeks ago." Juan Carlos recounted.

"It seems like longer. One long continuous bad memory. Strangeness lives on these streets. A numbing strangeness that feels wrong, like I should be somewhere else."

"It will be better after we climb the mountain."

"But how can I expect it to get better? Part of me will always be here and this place will always haunt me."

"Do not say that, Gabriela. We must trust that freedom from this tormented memory will come."

"My dear Juan Carlos, always the optimist. Beware of becoming the fool."

"I am more than aware of being tested Gabriela."

"But look at it my loyal suitor. This place will always bother me."

A compassionate point as they passed a small alley way filled with indigents. Tired looking men and women that littered the streets while occupying space previously reserved for dormant things that had no value in the world. Filthy vagrants that lived from deal to meal until they fell from existence.

Oppressed people too numerous for the limited space around them. Impoverished women with glazed eyes and broken spirits, sadly encircled by dirty faced children without stretched hands. Pitiful children that recklessly dodged traffic, while drunks threw dice and prostitutes peddled their wares.

They found themselves in a condemned place, where a spiritual river of life had been turned into a polluted grave. A squalid spring of oozing filth that was the home of a lecherous host. A Predatory Will of Addiction that hooked its prey, welcomed them to its lair and consumed their souls.

Becoming silent for the first time since finding each other, their echoing footsteps announced their presence. A presence that crept among shadows as Juan Carlos and Gabriela passed through many strange streets. Alcohol, Benzedrine, Cocaine, Dependency, Ecstasy, Fentanyl, Greed, Heroin, Illness, Jealousy, Killing, L.S.D., and Marijuana. They were in the heart of MooDooM.

A place of crumbling, soot covered buildings, where gangs patrolled and died with regularity. A regularity that left them uneasy as they rounded a corner and Gabriela stumbled on Marijuana Street. Grabbing Juan's arm to regain her balance, as a spray of loose gravel noisily pinpointed their location.

"That is the second time that you have saved me. How will I ever repay you?" Gabriela playfully chimed.

"Get us through this neighborhood and you can consider your debt forgiven." He whispered while scanning the streets.

"You must not worry Juan. If we are destined to make it through, then it will be so. If we are doomed for failure, then so it shall be."

"Be quiet!" Juan Carlos hushed.

A wasted warning for activity was awakening. Illuminated by crackling street fires, they watched as a threatening movement emerged from the shadows. Tracking the movement while planning a retreat, the emerging figures quickly encircled them. Twelve shadowy figures that moved to within five meters before revealing their faces.

Faces of children. Small, undernourished boys, some as young as ten and none of them older than fifteen. Bitter kids that marched about in a contrived fashion, implying an age far beyond their years. Hungry kids that were robbed of their childhoods, being forced to fight for their existence. A pitiful group from which a lanky boy came forth.

Easily the largest in the group, he stood about 5'8" weighing barely 130 pounds. A thin frame draped with dark skin that shined from exposure to filth. Filth that left his teeth blackened and his eyes reddened with anger. A dangerous young man barely into puberty, that sauntered to the front.

"Good evening Sir. I take it that all is well with you and the lady tonight."

"It is." Juan Carlos cautiously replied.

"Excellent. Perhaps you bring good news for me and my friends?  You see we were out for a walk, enjoying the sights amid the beauty of this moon lit night. And during the course of our evening jaunt, casually going about our business, we have become hungry. Do you know what it is like to be hungry during a late-night walk?" The boy bated.

"All too well I am afraid. These are very difficult times." Juan answered.

"I see. Well, that being the case, I assume that you are also aware that such hunger has the effect of lessening the enjoyment of the evening."

"I can say with absolute certainty, that a moon filled night can only be rightly appreciated with a full belly." Juan explained.

"Very interesting. We always get the most fascinating visitors on nights of the full moon. I take it from the words you speak and the women you hold, that you are a man of understanding. The type of man with considerable means, if you get my point?"

"Nay, my young friend for many things are not as they seem. While I may appear to possess qualities that you consider noteworthy, I can assure you that I am a man of very modest means."

"Ah, that is very unfortunate, for as you can see, we are many, haunted by the thought of food and burdened by a lack of cash. These being our troubling circumstances, we were hoping that you and the lady could help us with our problem. Perhaps a little something to help us on our way?"

Carefully watching the boy, Juan Carlos knew that something was seriously wrong. The boy exuded a sarcastic quality that bastardized his excessive politeness. A possessed quality that produced words not likely to come from a battered boy of the streets. However, seeing no reason in provoking him, Contraré calmly reached for one of his stashes of money. Cautiously removing the note from his trouser pocket, he crumpled the ten-dollar bill into a ball and tossed it to the boy.

"Sorry, there is not more, but that was my last ten dollars."

Snatching the money out of the air, the boy turned to the others as they greedily inspected their booty, amid a series of whispered remarks. Hushed phrases and belligerent innuendo they were about to unleash.

"We appreciate your assistance. But alas, we are plagued by a problem that remains. We are many and yet your offering is very small. Surely a man of your distinction can do better?" The boy asked.

"There is nothing I would like better, but as I said that was my last ten dollars. Perhaps you will have some luck further down the road." Juan answered.

"Perhaps." The boy strangely replied, as if speaking from some far away place.

Cognizant of a bad situation getting worse, Juan Carlos noticed that all of their eyes were glistening in the darkness.

A strange look of inebriation that left them looking bewildered. A drug filled stupor controlled by an Addictive Presence, that compelled them to utter words that were not their own.

"What about you fancy lady? Care to help out some hungry boys?" He asked Gabriela.

"Sorry, but he told you that is all we have."

"We heard what he said, but we don't like what it means!" He ranted.

"Well, we are sorry, but you cannot take what we do not have." She explained.

"Do not tell us what we can do!" The boy yelled.

"She tried to tell us what to do!" Another boy screamed.

The first of many responses with a decidedly hostile tone. Angry words with aggressive sneers as hatred swelled in their eyes. Hatred that possessed the boys with a contemptible propensity for violence. Hatred that transformed their postures into the insidious form of imprisoned children.

"We control this situation! Not you! We go where we want and we do as we please! Nobody tells us what to do! Got it?"

"She did not mean to offend you." Juan Carlos tried to explain.

"Shut up! Maybe we will take you women for a while. What do you think of that?"

Sadistic words and shrieking laughter, as the boys boiled from the wrath of that Addictive Force. Sacrificial souls that were under the control of a malicious spirit. An Addictive Will that assumed its form as the pure incarnation of evil.

Tension built to a feverish pitch as that Addictive Mood Of Doom seized control of their minds. Minds not to be trusted, because a knife in the hand of boy is just as deadly as a gun in the hand of a man.

Having recognized that their shuffling had placed them within striking distance, Juan Carlos took the opportunity and lunged at the largest boy, knocking him to the ground.

"Run!" He yelled while catching Gabriela's arm. A window of opportunity that provided an avenue of escape. Bolting onto a dark side street, the locked doors offered no refuge from the swarming boys. Boys that were hurling rocks and insults as they ran in pursuit.

"Get them! You're dead! You belong to me mother fucker! Pound the bastard! Your ass is mine you money loving bitch! Say goodbye asshole, your time has come!" They swore.

Barbaric insults that were accompanied by flying rocks that pelted their frames. A savage attack that brought them to their knees, when a large piece of rough concrete crashed into Gabriela's forehead. Badly dazed by the blow, she could not stand as a small stream of blood fused the boys with elation.

A dangerous situation as they huddled in a doorway for protection from the onslaught. Hatred dispensed by dangerous, drug crazed children. Juan Carlos considered firing a warning shot, but feared the boys may charge. Tottering close to armed action, Juan and Gabriela were saved by the shouts of approaching men.

The intrusion startled the boys into ceasing their attack. The silhouettes of three men with clinched fists and raised clubs were rushing toward them. Not prepared for another fight, the boys quickly retreated into the shadows. A place the men pursued as they attacked the shadows for the souls of the wayward boys. A righteous battle of broken glass and angry shouts that ended with pathetic pleas for mercy.

With the fight over, Juan Carlos turned his attention to Gabriela. Tenderly holding her face, he carefully inspected her wound. Using his dampened shirt sleeve to dot the cut, he said; "Nothing too serious. Just a flesh wound. A little soap and water and you will be fine."

"It sure felt like more than a flesh wound."

"How do you feel?" He asked.

"A little woozy, but I'm okay."

"Can you stand? We really should be moving on. Those three men could return." Juan warned.

"Do not worry. The one man is my friend." Gabriela announced.

"Your friend? How did you make a friend in a place like this?"

"I can make friends anywhere. It is my irresistible charm!"

"I see and how long have you known him?" Juan

pried.

"I am not good with time, but it seems as if I have always known him."

"Always?" Juan questioned.

"Yes, his name is Ray. Ray Light. He is an Angel that patrols these streets to spread Justice and Sobriety." Gabriela explained.

"An Angel in this town?"

"Sure, there are Angels everywhere. He died from an Addictive Situation. Some sort of drunk driving accident." She added.

"Such a shame when young people die before their time. So do you think you can stand?" Juan asked.

"I think so. Can you help me up? Oh, there he is. Hey Ray! What took you so long?" Gabriela yelled while steadying herself.

"That's my Ray on the right."

The three interceding men were emerging from the shadows. Healthy young men with white auras. Looking unscathed and confident, they were a breed apart from the rest of the locals.

"Those punks are getting brave. They normally run and hide, but tonight they wanted to fight. What did you do to get them so riled up?" Ray asked.

"Nothing Ray. We were just walking to my place, minding our own business, when they jumped us."

"Well, they won't be jumping anyone else for a while. We had to kick some ass, but I think they got the point. Hey what happened to you head Gabby?"

"Just a little scratch. Nothing serious Ray, thanks to my friend. Ray this is Juan Carlos."

"Pleased to meet you, Ray. I want to thank you for the help." Juan stated while extending his hand in greeting.

"You are welcome, but I cannot shake your hand. We are different. I am spirit and you are flesh. I patrol these streets with my colleagues. This is Justice and this is Temperance. We are trying to make a difference and we need you to make a difference?" Ray announced.

"Anything. How can I help?" Juan offered.

"Gabby needs you. She does not belong here. She is with child. You must love and care for her. Protect her and be patient with her. Can you do this?"

"I think so. Once I get her to the mountaintop, I can get her home.

Once home she will be fine." Juan explained.

"Do you know the way?"

"Yes, I can find The Bridge and we are still strong enough to get across."

"Good luck. Goodbye Gabby. Until we meet again." Ray spoke while turning to walk away.

"Goodbye Ray, I will never forget you!" Gabby spoke as her friend quietly disappeared into the shadows.

Turning to Juan she softly whispered; "Hold me, Juan Carlos! Please hold me!" And clinging to each other like warm bed sheets, their passionate embrace softened the despair that surrounded them.

———————○◇○———————

"This is home!" Gabriela announced as she opened a creaky door in an old building on Sex Street. Fumbling in the darkness to find a match, she soon brought the room alive. A sparsely furnished one room flat, adorned with a bed in the corner and a handleless dresser that stood next to an open window.

"Do you like it?" Gabriela asked as she moved to a water basin that lay atop the dresser.

"Not as bad as I thought. This might work." Juan Carlos remarked.

"What might work?" She asked while cleaning her face.

"I feel MooDooM's touch and smell his breath. He is strong here. We have a long climb to the mountain top, and I would feel better if you were stronger."

"I am fine, really I am! Show me the mountain and I assure you that I can climb it!" She insisted.

"I am not so sure, but I have an idea!" Juan suggested.

"Oh, I like ideas. Ideas are good for games. Can we play a game?"

"Of course, Gabriela, but this time by my rules."

"Anything you say Juan Carlos, but before we play, try this to help us on our way." Gabriela added.

So, Gabriela spread two lines of white powder on the

dresser. She snorted the first and Juan snorted the second. A powerful drug that numbed them to the world. Swooning with delight, their sensual union was fueled by unbridled passion and a powerful narcotic. Sex they intensified with a four-word mantra.

## *Sex Mantra*

"Look into my eyes and repeat to me.

What are you thinking? What are you thinking?

Keep doing it. What are you thinking? What are you thinking?

Don't stop! Do it faster!

What are you thinking? What are you thinking?

More! Faster! Longer!

What is he thinking? What is he thinking?

What is she thinking? What is she thinking?

And on and on and on!"

What is he thinking? What is she thinking? A simple axiom that contains a complex technique for shedding the limits of I'ness. A technique that enables some people with solvent propensities for concentration, to escape their singular perspectives by seeing the world through another's mind.

By repeating this axiom while intoxicated with powder, Gabriela and Juan Carlos found themselves delving deeper and deeper into their subconscious. Completely oblivious to the outside world, their minds quickly became blank transparencies. Receptive minds of sensitivity that were vulnerable divining rods for MooDooM.

Sometime during this period of psychological union, their tormented exploration was obscenely invaded by a groggy haze. Erupting from the River Addiction, an Addictive Spirit crept over a bridge that separated their withdrawal. A narcotic surge that seeped into every aspect of their beings while devouring their thoughts. An Addictive Spirit that poisoned their bodies, possessed their souls and ruled this place called MooDooM.

Numb to the world, Juan Carlos lost all contact with Gabriela. Rendered helpless in his torment, Juan was savagely lashed by MooDooM. An internal attack that shook his reason, ravaged his senses and commanded allegiance in his heart. Struggling to break the cycle of addiction, Juan Carlos yelled into the approaching Doom.

"Go! Return from whence ye came Oh Dark Knight of Pain! Leave me and the people that you haunt! Be gone for a new freedom burns bright in the hearts of those that reject your using ways!"

But only laughter returned. A tormented laughter of madness that cynically shook the foundation of his beliefs. Lost hope as addiction tried to render him obedient in a barren state of mindless mush. A savage violation that turned his MeoPian dialogue morose.

Why had this happened? He simply wanted to feel content. He never harmed anyone but himself, yet he now faces the prospect of being forever hooked. A state of addiction that soured his innocent thoughts until they no longer resembled their original form. Beautiful forms that he wasted on the solace of inebriation, under the daunting specter of MooDooM's shadow.

An act of experimentation that was sanctified by the promise of easy salvation. Snared by the trappings of exaltation, Juan Carlos exposed himself to a mortifying image that rendered him hooked and obedient. An addictive buzz that wound him with delight, before spinning him out of control. Drug induced aesthetic bliss, followed by a moment that wanted to repeat the first.

A muted state that left Juan aesthetically nurtured, but foolishly clumsy. A derelict state of over indulgence that transformed a happy young man into a psychological mess, neurotically driven by self- induced delirium. A grotesque state that dimmed his vision, stole the future and cracked his will as he fell.

Gradually regaining his self-control, Juan Carlos opened his eyes and found himself in the tormented underbelly of MooDooM. Turning his attention to Gabriela, he found her with an expressionless face that passively stared into space. An endless fixation for Gabriela had passed to the other side and nothing would resurrect her. She was dead. A martyr for the cause, a sacrifice to an unthankful ghost! An Eternal Goddess permanently entombed in these sacred pages.

Backing away while trembling with disbelief, Juan Carlos arose from the bed, donned his clothes and prepared to leave. But how to say goodbye? He was numbed by the reality of a bad dream turned obscene, as death claimed another victim in its crusade against the living.

My Dear Gabriela, you are my Mary Shelley. Please come back to me. Life is not the same without you. Please come back, I will do anything that you ask. Your obedient servant awaits your every command. It is no good without you. Please Zena, Gabriela is not taking orders. Come back, Oh God come back!" Juan Carlos wept.

Gabriela was gone. Never to return. A final kiss before they part. An enchanted kiss with the hope of magic.

"Goodbye Gabriela! When I regain my power, I will find you. I promise." He whispered. Preparing to leave, he turned to go, but was stopped by the future.

"Can I come along?" Overjoyed with the relief he cried.

"You are alive!"

"Of course, I'm alive. Did you think I was going to let this place get the better of me? You taught me better than that my love."

"But Gabriela, I thought you were dead."

"Gabriela is dead. I am Mary Shelley. Your old Mary Shelley and we have to get out of here."

"Oh Honey, you have no idea how long I have wanted to hear you say so."

"Tell me Contraré, how do we get out of MooDooM?"

"Our situation is desperate Mary Shelley, but not futile. There are many ways into MooDooM, but only one way out. Since we jumped from Alcohol to other drugs, we have a long journey for freedom. This journey will take us across all of MooDooM's tricks and pitfalls, as we stumble through the streets in search of the XYZ Bridge. Everyone enters through one of the 24 streets, but to leave all must cross the bridge."

"So, let's go!" Mary Shelley insisted.

"But what about your stuff?"

"Forget it. There is nothing here for me. I want to leave now!"

"So be it. Let us depart this tormented place for happier times."

And so, they departed that place to find a life they once knew. But their search for a dream was blocked by a ghostly presence that scurried about on the backs of rodents. An Addictive Urge that offered refuge in puke-stained doorways. Places they crossed while dodging cars and avoiding stares on the way to the promised land.

They crossed Overdose and Peyote Street. Rested on Quitters Street. They ran through Rehabilitation Street. They endured Sex, Tolerance and User Street, while sleeping on Valium Street. Withdrawal Street was the hardest, but they had enough and it was time to leave. No more games. Bring on the Bridge.

There is a bridge at the end at the end of XYZ Street. MooDooM patrols from the river under the bridge, offering temptation for those who wish to stay. Few make it this far and those that have are souls that MooDooM wished to keep. Focusing all of his Addictive Energy on this point, the bridge separates two contrasting lifestyles. They are worlds apart with the saved on one side and the condemned on the other. Salvation awaits those that successfully cross the bridge.

The bridge is rapidly crumbling from the persistent swat of abuse, so to cross it is a challenging task. MooDooM poisons the air with turmoil and punishes the road with decay. It is easy to fall through the numerous cracks by swaying the way that people do. Fledgling memories of how bad it is as you muddle between fulfillment and dereliction.

"Should we walk or run Contraré?"

"Too risky to run, but the less time we spend on the bridge the better. I will go first. You match my every step. If the bridge will hold my efforts, you will be safe. If I fall through, remember to stay away from the edge."

"Oh Contraré, you are not going to fall through."

"I know, but just in case. So how about a hug and a kiss?"

"How about it is right!" She exclaimed as they joined and started across the bridge. Moving slowly at first, they found the footing to be slippery but firm. Speeding up to get out of the air, they crossed the middle of the bridge and things started to improve. Once they could see the other side, they moved swiftly and with ease. Jumping from the bridge to the ground, they found themselves on the chosen shore. The privileged ones that had escaped the clutches of Addiction.

The mountain that Contraré descended, blocks this shoreline. To scale its peak is a rigorous climb and a sustained effort is needed. Slippages can put you back at the beginning and some people never complete the test. But Mary Shelley and Contraré were strong and committed.

Jointly determined to succeed, a slow but deliberate assent enabled them to make it. They had escaped MooDooM's lair and stood on the mountaintop. Having a moment to reflect on their ordeal, they looked back from whence they came and pondered the perils of their journey. A journey with still many tribulations ahead, for MooDooM has the enticing allure of following people wherever they may go!

### *End MooDooM*